HOW TO FEEL GOOD....EVEN WHEN I DON'T

A little book of Joy and Possibility for YOU!

Author: Su Owen

Illustrations: Jasmine England-Shave and Su Owen

That can make this hard to do but if we can just try together....

Let's close our eyes and just try to take a slow nice long deep breath in, try to breathe in all the way down to your tummy and now breathe out ....very slowly......and let's try to repeat this a couple of times, just to give us a moment of calm and space ....

Space to feel and if we aren't feeling Good let us try together to help change that ....

Sit or lie in a comfortable position.... put one hand on your belly and one hand on your chest .... now .....

Take a deep breath in through your nose or mouth and let your belly push your hand out....

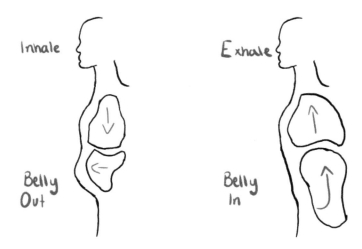

Breathe out through your mouth as your belly goes in and your chest relaxes....and let go....and repeat over and over....

You can do this it can just take a little practise.

Let's think like we are blowing up a balloon inside us with our breath....by pushing out our tummy on our in breathe and pulling our tummy in on our out breath....you can also pause here and look it up on the internet if you wish to, always best to do this with a trusted adult.

So why do we have all these thoughts and emotions and feelings?

Why? ....What are they really? ....

My thoughts and feelings are energy.... energy is vibration ....

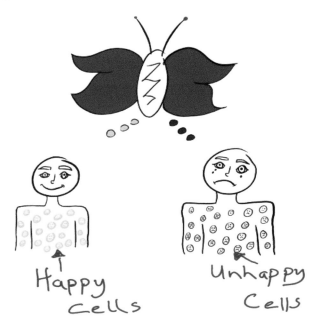

Happy Cells

Unhappy Cells

The way we look at something, our perception, changes how that FEELS!

And as we are energy and vibration.... this has an effect on us ....

You may enjoy listening to a happy little song each day....there is a nice one on you tube called "every little cell in my body is happy"....always look things up with a trusted adult....

We do all have a lot of different thoughts and feelings, even in just one day!

Thoughts create emotions and feelings, so if we have an unhappy thought it could easily make us feel sad or angry or many more negative emotions.

Our thoughts and emotion are energy.... and energy is vibration....and energy can

and does change.... so our emotions and
vibration can change.....

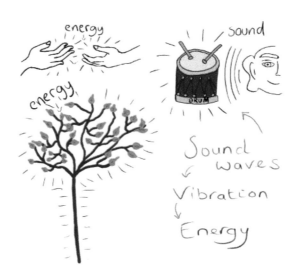

We are energy....we are vibration....
the Whole Universe is vibration, vibrating
at different frequencies....

So how does knowing that help Us?

We are feeling sad because someone said
something ....
Something happened........

We are feeling sad, angry, unhappy ....

Because our feelings are our guide in all
this, we can change our thoughts, which
can help change our energy and vibration ....

Here we have, 1 happy person thinking
"I feel happy another new day, the rain
helping the planet and life to flourish"....
1 sad person thinking "I feel miserable
another cold and wet day"

As we can see in this simple drawing, how we look at things, our perspective can change everything!

If we can know that nothing is more important than that we FEEL GOOD this can help guide us through our FEELINGS.

Now it can seem hard to change a disagreement, an unkind action, or unkind words, but if we really want to feel better, we have to be able to allow ourselves to let go and take a different look (perspective) at how we choose to FEEL.

Please note: if any child reading this book has worries about anyone's behaviours towards them please always ask a responsible trusted adult for help.

Remember...... we are energy and vibration ......let's choose not to give away our energy on arguing who is right, even if it is us!

Let's choose to FEEL GOOD ....

It could be that the person who affected our feelings is not actually feeling good or very happy themselves and they may have things going on that we do not know about and they are unable to be happy and kind at this moment.

So often their actions or words are actually coming from fear

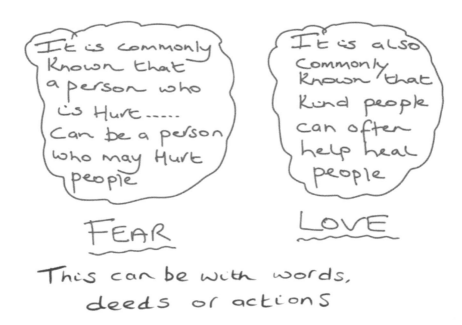

FEAR   LOVE

This can be with words, deeds or actions

Now, this is where we can decide to be kind anyway. This is where we can decide to let go and be peaceful towards them anyway. This has been a practise by great peacemakers of the world throughout history, deciding to practise ....Love, Peace and Kindness ....

Now I know this is sounding like a lot of serious stuff.... but actually it is much easier than we think ....

The great peacemaker Mahatma Gandhi believed change starts with each one of us. He believed we could all become the change we wished to see in the world.... because as we change, so does everything else.

(The Peace Mudra is a simple hand gesture ....simply let our left hand rest gently in our right hand with thumbs softly touching, and breathe....and allow....we can allow ourselves to feel peace....)

Peace Mudra

Mahatma Gandhi

Martin Luther King Jnr.

This was echoed by another amazing peacemaker Martin Luther King Jnr. Who believed we could all become the peace we wished to see in the World.

This really can be adopted by all of us to bring kindness, peace and love into our lives and to help take our feelings to a much better place.

The big thing for us to know is there are only 2 emotions behind all emotions....Fear and Love....and we can for sure feel each of them, even though it does seem there are far more!

Let us just stop again for a moment and think of something that made us really happy, remember...and now FEEL.... hopefully that will connect us to a good feeling....

We did that with our thoughts and imagination....well done....we are amazing!

That is the power of our thoughts, feelings and energy....we just changed our vibration to a happier one!

We will be aware of energy and vibration much more than we realise....our feelings are always our guide....

So, let's look at a day at school, for example, and our feelings....we could arrive at school after a lovely walk there, seeing beautiful trees and hearing the birds, meeting our friends and Feeling Good already!

Or....

We may have had an argument at home, a family fall out, or someone sent an unkind text and we arrived at school a little late too....and now we feel anxious, unhappy and not very good....

If we are the one feeling good, we can find it easier to be more kind and peaceful towards others.

Sadly, if we are the one not feeling so good that may even make us be unkind to someone.

This is where we can decide to practise random acts of kindness anyway!!

And if we are the not feeling good today kid, let us try to help together.....

So we know thoughts become things because we are feeling a whole lot of unpleasant things right now....ok, now let us go back to the breathing exercise....let us now take time to take our thoughts to a better feeling place....

This is where our imagination can really help us.

Ok we cannot change in this moment what happened or what was said but we can Change how we Feel about it!

The Truth is I can do this, Me, Awesome Amazing ME!

CHAPTER 2

So awesome Me still wants to FEEL GOOD....

Let us start at the beginning of our day....

The start of a brand new everything....
or is it? Really?

We really do create our own reality, each day, starting with our thoughts! So why don't we try to make today the best it can be for us, starting right now!

Yawn!!! We are waking up!

But let's take our first few moments, not to reach for a device (phone/tablet/TV) or let our thoughts of the day ahead race away....let us just breathe....a nice long deep calming breath....as we did in chapter 1....

let's do this for a few moments.

Now we don't want to let our thoughts shoot off on a negative track....so we can now create happy thoughts for this bright new day....even if it is dull and raining....

Still focusing on these nice calming breaths have a nice stretch through our body from the top of our head to the tips of our toes.

Give a happy thought of appreciation for our amazing body that breathes for us, and completes so many incredible tasks in so many ways every day for US!

We could just allow ourselves to think of our favourite animal, as they wake up to a new day .... what do they do? What is their pattern and flow?

What they do is go to THEMSELVES, what do they need in this moment, a nice stretch, a drink, a bit of fresh air....they don't reach for a device....they bring themselves back into a new day ....

So if we can change how we wake up and step into each new day we will be changing our energy and vibration ....

This is also a great chance for us to let go of what we usually do, and definitely not go straight to the habit of picking up a device or turning on a TV ....we can choose to change.... because we want to Feel Good....

Ok so now why don't we take another few minutes to use our incredible imagination to see and feel our day as we wish it to be....remember it is the Feeling Good here that matters.

Our imagination is everything, so why not start each day setting it up as we wish it to be!

I know it's easy to think things like that unkind person at school will still be there or that I still even have to go to school.... but hang on, let's not forget our own amazing power....to change thoughts .... energy ....vibration....to feel good anyway.

It is not just superheroes that have amazing power, so do WE!!

We now know we have the power to change our thoughts ....and we do want to feel good right?

So today, as we take a few waking moments to breathe and stretch we could also use our awesome powers to imagine our day ahead, and feel it ....

We can also take a moment to appreciate US, to look in that mirror and say 'good morning .... I do Love You and we are going to have a good feeling day today ....'

Umm....that seems odd doesn't it, looking in a mirror to say 'I Love You' ....but when we can do it and feel it without picking on ourselves....like we may usually complain at our looks in a mirror ....

But this is a new everything we are starting right here....and Loving Ourselves is the most important thing of all....

If we have love for ourselves it is easier to love others....it really is!
Because as we feel good about ourselves, we will be able to see the love in others.... even when they may not be being the best they can be all of the time ....

We can appreciate our beautiful new day, so what if it is raining and windy, it really is still a beautiful new day for us, awesome US!

We can be thankful for so many things that we may not have just quite appreciated before ....our bed, our comfy cosy bed, lovely warm bedding, our room, our home, our family, ...umm we may not have quite thought like this before but it is beginning to help with feeling good ....

This could be how we now start our day ....ok it is feeling good .....let's try not to be distracted by looking at a phone, or device, or TV, let's focus on setting up our feeling good day ....

Let's start with our new perspective, our new way of looking at things and starting our brand new day ....

We can start our new day with some simple happy exercises...let's wake up those happy cells .....

Let's take our fingertips and start tapping gently on our head, down to our toes and back up a few times....and then gently twist from our hips swinging our arms and moving our feet....and finally give our arms, legs and body a nice happy shake out, all over ....just allowing our beautiful body to wake up to a bright new day....

Tap all over

Shake out

Twist and Turn and move..

We could now just take a few minutes to sit comfortably, close our eyes, and use our imagination to visualise our day ahead, breathing slowly, feeling into good feeling thoughts for the day.

We can go to school looking at things that make us feel good, we can appreciate nature, its elements, its beauty in the trees, the sky, just look at that sky ....rain clouds or sun....it is all full of wonder ....

Actually, just thinking about nature, wow it is pretty awesome isn't it? All of its different elements, its incredible beauty, and it surrounds us, we just sometimes pass it by without even realising....

So let's feel into that...but it is raining... yeah....but my skin is waterproof!!....and look at all the good that comes from rainfall.

We all need the rain and nature flourishes, but my thoughts are now going to floods ....ok yes we know they do happen, but eventually they also subside and nature does its amazing work again to recover ....

So, let's keep focusing on our good feeling thoughts ....We are still on our way to school and we are feeling love for ourselves and appreciating things like never before ....

So, as we arrive at school, we can choose to still keep feeling good, no matter what....

We haven't even bothered with our phone yet, we were enjoying our new day and just allowing ourselves to Feel Good ....

We could even feel inspired now to make some great suggestions at school, it would be so nice to have maybe a white board in class where we could all simply put notes for the day on how we are feeling as we arrive ....

Ours could be, we are feeling happy, for some it maybe they are feeling sad or angry. This could help all of us practise random acts of kindness anyway and help each other.

For if we remember to be kind anyway, without judging the other person, simply observing that they are not feeling good our kindness could help.

And if we also remember that if their reaction is not a good one, we do not have to react, we can just respond with love and kindness.

Some schools have a naughty table or corner, which can even make us feel worse....but if we could change that to a peace table or peace corner, with the chance to reflect and choose peacefully how to resolve any issues....it could help everyone....we can look these up on the internet....and who knows we may be able to help make a change in our own school to having a peace table or peace corner.

Let's remember, is it more important to be right? Or is it more important to let it go and Feel Good?...we want to Feel Good....

If we keep our good feeling energy going, we will not be the only ones that feel it....

If we can remember to agree to disagree, peacefully, no matter what, and we know that is going to be hard, but we really do want to Feel Good!!

If we can accept that whatever it is, it is what it is, and if we can allow it to just be and let it go we will Feel free .....

CHAPTER 3

However, we know we are energy and vibration ....and we know that our thoughts become things, both positive and negative ....something may happen, it could be something huge or a simple unpleasant comment, either on social media or verbally, but our feeling response may be really massive....because no matter what the situation or cause is....our emotions do not care about what the experience is ....

So, our emotions do not care about what the experience is, so if we get an unkind comment, we could experience horrendous sadness, fear and anger, whilst someone else would not be impacted at all by the same situation ....

Hold on what exactly does that mean?

So we have an emotional reaction ....to an experience, and how we think about that experience or situation will result in our feeling response, just like the picture.

When we experience an emotion, say sadness, anger, the way it affects us could be huge, or it could have no effect on another person....our emotions do not care how big the negative experience is, the way we perceive it to be will be what triggers our feelings....

If we take a few moments to actually feel into a happy thought, we will feel that energy in our body, it may be goose bumps it may be a happy feeling in our tummy .... but if we feel into a sad thought, the energy we feel here will be very different, it may cause us to feel anxious and have an unpleasant feeling of energy in our body ....our thoughts are really that powerful!!!!

Let's FEEL into ᵒᵒᵒHappy

Let's FEEL into Sadᵒᵒ

By allowing ourselves to FEEL those thoughts we become aware that they do FEEL different in our body.

So if we can use all the tools we have already in this little book ....along with a new one we will introduce here....we can start to change our emotional responses to things ....

Let's go back to our breath every time to start with ....this can help calm us down and be in each moment of now ....now right here using our breath and hopefully being able to change our focus to a better feeling thought ....

We woke up this morning as a new US, taking time for us to stretch and ease our way into a better feeling day BUT ....right now we can't get back to that better feeling place so let's try something else to help us ....

This is a simple technique called Tapping or E.F.T. Emotional Freedom Technique....it is quite simple and can be really helpful and effective ....we use our fingertips to tap on parts of our body to help reduce stress and negative feelings....

So, we are going to tap on a few points, as seen on the drawing ....if we follow the numbers on the drawing, and the list, they will help us .....

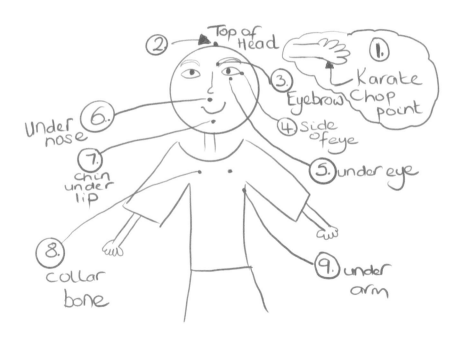

We are going to gently 'tap' on the points from the side of our hand, which is called the karate chop point....to the top of our head, to the eyebrow, side of the eye, under the eye, under the nose, chin point in the middle, collarbone spot and under the arm ......if we follow the diagram it is not as hard as it seems!!!!

So, the order is....

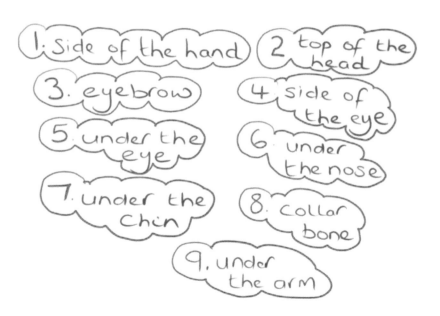

We start on the side of the hand, the KC Karate chop point, either hand, and tap with opposite fingers....let's say we are angry because someone said something unkind ....so we start with a set up statement....and we remember self-love for US ....so we could say something like ....

'Even though I am really mad at what they said, I love and accept myself....' (if it is still hard to say we love ourselves we could try 'I am willing to allow love for myself....') keep tapping on this point....

'Even though they should not be unkind, I love and accept myself'

Repeat and feel this a few more times then move to the next point....the top of the head....your statement may change just feel....it could be something like 'even though I feel angry' ....the words you use

will be unique to you ....just tap on each
point a few times and move on .....so from
the top of the head to the eyebrow point....
then the side of the eye....under the eye....
under the nose....the chin....the collar bone...
under the arms....and back to the top of
the head....this is one round of tapping .....

Repeat as needed and allow yourself to
feel a little ease on each round....and as you
change how you feel your wording will
change ....

Most important in this is, you can't get it
wrong....just really allow your breath and
your feelings to guide you....the words you
use will all be guided by your feelings and
your breath will soothe you if you allow
it....

We could write a whole chapter on this
amazing tool to help you but we won't ....

we will trust YOU and if you want to use EFT please look it up on the internet .....
at this trusted site who also take tapping into schools to help children and teachers ....www.tappingsolution.org and www.tappingsolution.com

How we look at things does matter, how we respond to things does, but we have more control of this now, don't we? We can do this because our feelings are our guide ....

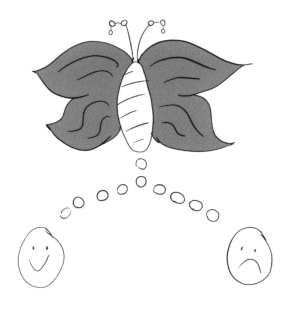

Let's allow ourselves to accept exactly how we feel right now, in this moment ....we may have felt either Love or Fear about some situation ....well actually a whole bunch of emotions that can only ever be Love or Fear and we now want to focus on getting ourselves to a good feeling place, by letting go....

Oh, just another reminder here....we are the smartest person we know!!!!

If we can choose to use some of these simple ideas to help us through each day .... making small changes that Feel better... we will Feel the difference ....

And at the end of each day if we decide to reflect on our day by going to bed in an attitude of gratitude for the good things of each day and letting go of anything else ....we will Feel different....

We may even want to make few happy changes to our bedroom, make things a little different....how about a few beautiful house plants....we can care for them and benefit from them....they are energy and energy is vibration, remember ....

Let's make sure we have pictures and music that make us feel happy which are special to US....we could make a space for us to stretch and move as we awake and before we go to bed too....just little things that help us to Feel Good ....

We know adults are always on about keeping our room tidy and no clutter... but everything is energy ....and if we can create a calm peaceful room....with space, light, nature, happy pictures...that is all going to help us Feel better ....

And at the end of our day....let's choose... balance....choose how we feel going to bed this will change how we feel when we wake up!!!

Remember if we Feel into a happy thought, and we allow....we can experience Feeling Good but if we Feel into say, a sad thought, we can experience not feeling good ....

One is high vibration and one is low vibration....as we know we are energy and vibration ....

If 'The Truth is today was a good day' .... we will Feel it .....
Just as we will if our statement that.... 'The Truth is today was a bad day' ...... we can let go of anything that did not Feel good and focus on the things that did!!!! We can fill in our thoughts to remind us!

CHAPTER 4

You know we just mentioned plants in your bedroom, that may sound weird to us but hang on ....let's make this chapter a happy reminder to us about the magnificence of nature...in all its forms .....

Connecting with nature can really help our feelings ....

Now we are not going to say we should all go out and hug a tree right now ....although you may be happily surprised if you do!!!!

But actually, being with nature in so many different ways can really help us to feel good.....so let's do it .....

We may or may not have a garden, or there may be a local park or similar areas of nature close by ....we could take some time to literally just stand in nature.... close to a tree perhaps or other forms of nature ....

We may live in an area surrounded by nature or in a very busy area with very little nature ....but if we really look carefully, umm there may be trees on pathways and small parkland areas we have not noticed before, we may be lucky enough to have a nice garden....any way to connect will give us the chance to hopefully feel better...and see and appreciate nature in a whole new way.

If we look at a tree, which stands, often very firm and grounded no matter what goes on around....it adapts to all the changes of the seasons....it does it all anyway .....

So if we can take some time to even connect with the sounds of the birds daily, the nature that surrounds us in all its various forms, to allow ourselves to stop and feel and appreciate....the beauty, the fascination of how it all just allows .... every day ....every change .....we may find ourselves feeling more grounded and connected....and feeling better...walking in nature has always been a wonderful way to relax and connect ....we could all try this in whatever way feels best for us....

As we take time to just really allow ourselves to be right here in this moment with nature we could just stand

and breathe and allow ourselves to feel
energy....and we will feel it....just take our
time with our breath and allow ....and
feel....

For if we begin to see and appreciate
nature in a whole new way, we will feel
differently, for the better....

Our environment and how we treat it is so important and we can be a big part of helping our planet and environment in many ways.

Some schools have their own Eco Councils, with students who are able to look at how they can all help reduce waste, do more re-cycling, create their own vegetable gardens within the school, so many possibilities and good feeling projects to be part of ....

We could be part of a local Incredible Edibles project which grows vegetables for our community, for free, in un-used areas of land ....many towns already do this, with children helping too ....

Growing our own food is much nicer than you may think....as all food we eat has a big effect on how we feel and our mood.

Our amazing body can sometimes react to many processed foods and drinks which often have many chemicals and huge amounts of sugar.

If we become aware of how we feel after eating things this will really help to guide us in our lives, and eating local and home-grown food will often give us energy we only thought was possible from a sugary processed energy drink!!

Allow yourself to feel into this ....

Nature and its possibilities are endless .... nature is energy and vibration and we will feel this as we connect to nature around us ....

Nature also provides many natural healing flowers and herbs which have been used over hundreds of years to help people in so many ways ....

There are some very simple remedies which were created in the 1930's ....a long time ago.....by a doctor as a natural way of helping our emotions and feelings....

These are the Bach Flower Remedies, and Rescue Remedy is a very good all round remedy to help in times of stress, shock and anxiety, which we can all feel at sometimes....

We could look them up on the internet, always best to do this with a trusted adult ....they are very simple to take and can really help to bring us ease at difficult times .....

These could be another helpful tool for us along with our breath work, and E.F.T. tapping at times ....

when we feel we need them ....

Please note: Nature is amazing but do not eat any wild flowers without expert guidance from a trusted adult.

All Bach Flower Remedies and other plant-based remedies are only prepared by qualified, trusted adults.

CHAPTER 5

We already are aware of being energy and vibration....and we know there have been times when we have had an inner feeling about something, either good or bad, often we feel it in or around our tummy area .... just feeling if something is right or not ....

We are going to just feel into this and if it doesn't feel right for us that is fine too.... we can always come back to this or just leave it for now ....

So by now we have actually got a pretty good idea that everything is about Feeling ....

And it is very likely that most of us have, at times, had a Feeling or Knowing that made us feel safe and not alone ....this may even have been described to us by adults as maybe a Guardian Angel or something similar... although most of us have at some time had a feeling or an awareness of help and guidance we have been given and we weren't really sure....

Well actually this is really not far from the Truth....

The Truth is we are never alone, even in our hardest of times, because we do have a connection to our Higher Self....

Our What??

Our Higher Self can be thought of as energy, vibration, the non-physical, friend who has always been with us....

What is Non-Physical?? It is energy, it is vibration, that we cannot normally see, but we can feel. There are some people who can see non-physical energy and we may be one of those ....but we can ALL FEEL.

Just hold on....this is all sounding strange to some of us, whilst some of us will actually know we have had experiences of perhaps....Feeling that someone was with us, maybe ....

This is like ....our best friend who is always with us ....we can use simple ways of trying to tune in to them, but only if we want to and we can let our feelings be our guide at all times....

We can set an intention to make it fun .... the thing is to be relaxed, calm and allowing....and of course Feel....

Again if any of this feels too strange for us we can just leave this, we must go with only what feels right for us....

Let's use our breath to bring us right here into this moment, slow deep relaxing breaths which allow us to be here and now, without racing thoughts....just a focus on our breath....

And as we allow this gentle focus we can set our intention to connect with the energy of our Higher Self....we may feel energy around us....the key is to relax and allow....keeping simple focus and allowing.... we may feel inspired by a name....which we can write down....everyone's Higher Self has a name....or we may just feel a lovely sense of peace and calm..

We would also guide you to far more help with the Higher Self at this Trusted and Safe website....

www.5thdimensionearth.com to The Higher Self Free Programme.... and in the book by Olivia and Raf Ocana called Believe ....

CHAPTER 6

So here we are the last chapter of this little book ....and we want to say THANK YOU for getting this far!!!

Just as a quick reminder of what you can now use, each day, to help you Feel Good

Firstly, and always our breath
Deep, slow, long breaths
We are energy and vibration .....
The way we look at things changes how we FEEL .....
Actions and words come from either LOVE or FEAR .....
Is it more important to be right or to let go and FEEL good .
Our imagination can really help us!!

We can change how we look
at things and how we FEEL...
We can change how we start
and end our day.......
We can learn to LoVE ourselves...
When we LoVE ourselves it
is easier to LoVE others ☺
We can resolve conflict peacefully...
We can appreciate and enjoy
nature more.....
We can use simple ideas in
this book to help us.......

Let's use these few pages to remind
ourselves how amazing we are....and of the
moments of joy in our lives ....

My Moments of Joy .....

My Moments of Joy .....